THE BIG
BOOK OF
MAGIC

Gyles Brandreth

Illustrated by Peter Stevenson

A CAROUSEL BOOK

RANSWORLD PUBLISHERS LTD.

Other books by GYLES BRANDRETH

1000 FACTS: THE GREATEST BOOK OF AMAZING
INFORMATION EVER KNOWN
1000 JOKES: THE GREATEST JOKE BOOK EVER
KNOWN
1000 RIDDLES: THE GREATEST BOOK OF RIDDLES
EVER KNOWN
1000 QUESTIONS: THE GREATEST QUIZ BOOK EVER
KNOWN
THE BIG BOOK OF OPTICAL ILLUSIONS
THE BIG BOOK OF PRACTICAL JOKES
JOKES! JOKES! JOKES! A JOKE FOR EVERY DAY OF
THE YEAR
THE DAFT DICTIONARY
THE BIG BOOK OF SECRETS
THE CRAZY ENCYCLOPAEDIA
THE CRAZY WORD BOOK
CRAZY DAYS
CHALLENGE
THE CRAZY BOOK OF WORLD RECORDS
SHADOW SHOWS

all published by CAROUSEL BOOKS

THE BIG BOOK OF MAGIC

A CAROUSEL BOOK 0 552 54177 X

First publication in Great Britain

PRINTING HISTORY
Carousel edition published in 1981
Carousel edition reprinted 1982
Carousel edition reprinted 1983 (twice)

Text copyright © Gyles Brandreth 1981
Illustrations copyright © Transworld Publishers 1981

Carousel Books are published by
Transworld Publishers Ltd.,
Century House, 61-63 Uxbridge Road,
Ealing, London W5 5SA.

Printed and bound by The Guernsey Press Co. Ltd., Guernsey,
Channel Islands.

Some
DOs
and
DON'Ts
by way of
INTRODUCTION

TEN DOs AND DON'Ts

DO rehearse

You must **practise** each
trick until it works every
time you do it. If you're
a good magician things
can go slightly wrong in
a trick without the au-
dience noticing you
putting them right. If
you're not sure of a
trick you will fumble.

   This book should be easy to use—all you have
to be able to do is read! It's set out so that you can
see at once what equipment, or bits and pieces,
you'll need for each trick, if any, what happens in
each trick, then how the trick is done. This way,
you'll have some idea of the sort of effect the magic
produces before you know the secret.

A trick marked with
this symbol means
that you need an
accomplice...

2

Each trick is graded on a
scale of difficulty:

Easy   Not so Easy   Not Easy

It's easy to miss something important when you
read a trick for the first time. It might seem a bit
of a waste of time to keep reading a trick again
and again, but really it's quicker than trying to
do a trick you haven't understood.

Even so, some tricks do not seem to make sense
however many times you read the secret! If this
is the case, don't skip the trick, but try it out.
You'll be surprised to find how easy it is when you
actually do it: it may seem so simple that you won't
know how you failed to grasp it the first time.

If you have a trick like this, one which seems
almost too simple ever to fool an audience, remember that people watching will be as puzzled
as you were when you first read the trick. As long
as you don't repeat bits of magic, very few people
spot how a thing is done the first time they see it.

DO plan for disasters

One day, you're on stage and a glass of water falls over soaking the pound note in your trouser turn-up. As you bend down to pick up the glass, coins and cards fall from your jacket and two sugar lumps slip from your top pocket into the spilt water and dissolve before your very eyes...

With a little luck, this will remain no more than a magician's nightmare! But it's still good sense to plan for when things go wrong. For instance, when disaster strikes you could tell a story or a joke about things going wrong. Or you might quickly go on to a simple trick that works every time. You might say, 'Well, I can't do this trick today—the weather's not right—so I'll stand on my head instead!' and stand on your head, if you can, before going on to the next trick in your show.

DO plan the patter

People on the radio seem to chatter away without thinking but even they plan some of what they say. To give yourself confidence and to make the show flow, write out a few things to say with each trick, and—once you know the trick—try it out with the patter. It's better to say **some**thing while you're performing rather than let the audience sit in silence. All audiences get bored very quickly if there's nothing happening and they expect magic shows to zip along with something exciting going on all the time. So, if you've run out of patter, just

5

say:

6

Everyone expects to hear the expressions they know, so when you get to the climax of a trick don't forget such golden oldies as '**Hey presto!**' and '**Abracadabra!**'

Do arrange your show

People get tired of seeing the same sort of trick over and over again. Perhaps you like card tricks more than other sorts of trick? Well, you can still do a few, but do **other** tricks in between—a trick with a coin, a trick with dice, a trick with glasses or some number magic. Apart from making up your patter you can think about how to arrange the stage so it becomes **yours**, and how to arrange your bits and pieces to make the stage an **arena of magic**. You could have a tablecloth with moons and stars on it; a big top hat; a wand. All the coins, glasses, cards, dice etc should be arranged on the table in the order in which you're going to use them.

7

When you make up the order of tricks for the show, remember to do not only different sorts of magic but also to change the mood. You might begin with a few quick, simple tricks, then do something which involves the audience, then do a jolly trick, then something serious and work towards your 'Grand Finale'—the best trick you can do. If you find that the audience gets restless before the end, don't torture them by sticking firmly to your programme—drop a few tricks and go on to your last and best. The audience will tire quickly however good you are, so don't think you've failed if they start fidgeting after what seems a short time. As long as you do the tricks well they'll enjoy the show—but don't force magic on them when what they'd really like is a good cup of tea!

The good magician knows just
when to disappear!

DON'T keep trying a trick that fails

If a trick goes wrong, you might have a second go but if it fails then, go on to something simple and good very quickly. Some magicians add to the excitement **deliberately** making mistakes, when they do a trick for the first time, but this isn't a good idea until you're a master magician: the trick may go wrong by accident the second time and then you're really in a mess!

**DO have tricks
for troublemakers**

You might get someone in the audience who thinks he's seen it all before. If he becomes a nuisance, get him up on stage and give him something impossible to do. He'll find that suddenly he's all alone, and probably looking very silly. He'll be glad to get back to his seat and sit quietly!

As you look through **THE BIG BOOK OF MAGIC** you'll find several tricks which are specially good for giving to the rowdy spectator. Watch out for the joker.

DON'T be too adventurous

You can do exciting and amazing things without
performing underwater or hanging from a burning
rope. Things that are really very simple often seem
astonishing to people who do not know the secret.
The best magician is the one who can make even
the simplest tricks seem utterly amazing.

DON'T reveal your secrets

Once others know the secret behind an illusion, it stops being an illusion. Magicians **never** reveal their secrets!

DON'T forget to entertain

Enjoy yourself and
be a happy magician.
You're putting on a
show so **SMILE**!
Crack some jokes!
Make your patter
snappy! And make
sure that a good
time is had by one
and all!

And lastly, but certainly not least,

DON'T PANIC!

You need a bit of nerve to go in front of an audience
by yourself and perform, but think of the magic
as there to help you. Remember that many of the
tricks you will be performing have come down from
the great masters of the past.

Once you've done the first couple of items you'll
find the magic will take over. If you still feel nervous, have an assistant with you all the time: it's
reassuring to have someone else on stage, and
many professionals have one or more assistants
by them throughout their show.

Get the audience to join in as much as you can, but remember that when you show them something you mustn't let them get too near the action—otherwise they'll want to inspect everything closely, and that's something you want to avoid! Keep the audience on your side by involving them, and they'll enjoy the magic even more.

Remember that practice really **does** make perfect—and if you really know what you're doing there will be no need to panic.

Happy conjuring!

MAKING A WAND

For some of your tricks, you'll need a **magic wand**. You can buy one at a magic shop, but in most towns the real trick is finding a magic shop! There are some famous ones in London (you will find their addresses in the Yellow Pages), but not many elsewhere.

It will probably be easier and cheaper for you **to make your own wand** rather than go and buy one.

Find a round stick. It should be about 1.2cm thick and 30cm long. It should be fairly smooth already, but sandpaper any bumps so it's completely smooth and rounded. Paint it with a black enamel glossy paint. Leave it to dry.

To get the ends white, put masking tape on the stick 2.5cm from each end. Paint the ends with white enamel. When this is dry, you can remove the masking tape leaving clear white edges and a perfect magic wand.

THE WAND IN THE MATCHBOX

Equipment:
    1 wand
    1 matchbox

What happens: When you perform this trick it will need to be the first one in your act. You come on stage holding a matchbox in your right hand. You open it. It contains your wand, all of which you pull out of the matchbox!

How it's done: You need a trick match-box. Remove the drawer from an ordinary matchbox. Cut out a space in one of the narrower ends just big enough for the wand to go through:

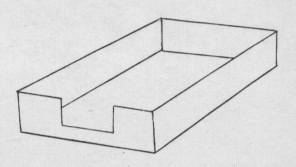

Put the drawer back in the box, and put one end of the wand into the box. The rest of the wand should be **hidden by your hand and up your coat sleeve.**

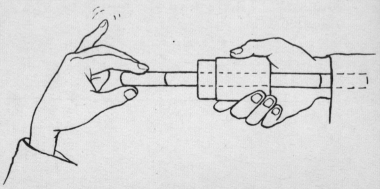

HELLO— AND GOODBYE!

Equipment:
  1 pair of white gloves
  2 lengths of elastic

What happens: This is another splendid little trick with which to begin your show. As you arrive on stage, you bow to your audience and say: **'Good Evening, Ladies and Gentlemen. It's a great pleasure to be with you this evening...'** As you do this, take off your gloves. They will immediately vanish!

How it's done: Sew one end of the elastic length to the inside of the glove. Attach the other end to the inside of your jacket with a small safety pin. Do the same with the other glove. You will have to experiment with the best position for the safety pin, but when the gloves shoot up your sleeve, it is best if the fingertips are 8-10 centimetres up the sleeves, so they cannot work themselves down again at any stage.

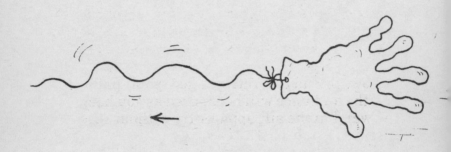

If you're worried about the safety pins, or feel uncomfortable with the gloves up your sleeves, you can take your jacket off after the first or second trick.

LOOK—NO FINGERS!

Equipment:
　　1 wand

What happens: You show the audience your wand. You can let them examine it so they can see that it hasn't been tampered with.

Now you lay it flat against your palm, and the audience will be amazed as you keep the wand in the air, apparently without support.

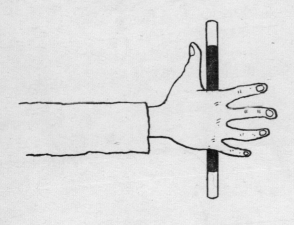

How it's done: The traditional way of doing this is to use the forefinger of your right hand to support the wand while the rest of your hand grips your left wrist. The audience will probably be deceived into thinking that all of your fingers are around your wrist. However, it's more convincing if you can hide a ruler in your sleeve and use it to hold the wand in position. In this way, all the fingers of your right hand are round your left wrist.

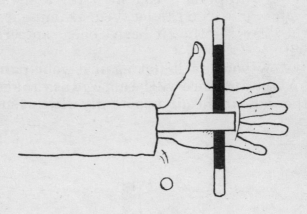

THE MAGIC EGG

Equipment:
    1 hard boiled egg
    1 egg cup

What happens: You tell the audience that you're going to make the egg fly. They won't believe you, but you can do it!

How it's done: Put the small end of the egg into the egg cup. Bring the egg cup close to your mouth and blow hard into the egg cup between the egg and the cup. If you blow hard enough the egg will fly from the cup. This is because there is so much air in the cup that it will push out the egg so it can escape.

MAGIC MIND-READING

Equipment:
None.

What happens: You choose an assistant from the audience. He blindfolds you and leads you outside. Your assistant asks someone from the audience to write down any number from **1 to 20** and to show him and the rest of the audience the number. The assistant then leads you back to the stage. You place your hands on either side of his forehead, that is, on his temples.

You say, **'I am getting messages through my hands. I can feel something ... yes ... the number is ...'.** Then you give the correct number.

How it's done: The 'assistant' is really an accomplice. He tells you the number by clenching his teeth slowly and firmly. You should be able to feel each time he does this, and he should be able to do it with the smallest amount of jaw movement, so the audience cannot see what's going on. If he clenches his teeth once, the number is one. If he does it twice it's two, and so on.

CHIN—CHIN!

Equipment:
   2 glasses

What happens: You fill one glass with water, and put another identical glass on top of it. You ask if there is anyone in the audience who is able—like yourself—to drink the water in the bottom glass without touching either glass with the hands.

How it's done: You pick up the first glass by getting hold of it between your chin and chest. You can now drink the water in the bottom glass by making the glass lean towards you:

THE FLOAT

Equipment:

1 wand

What happens: You wave your wand around to show it's quite normal, then hold it with your left hand against the palm of your right hand. When you take your left hand away, the wand stays where it is.

How it's done: You put two small pins in the wand a small distance apart. They shouldn't show above your hand, but you should be able to hold the wand by pressing your fingers against them.

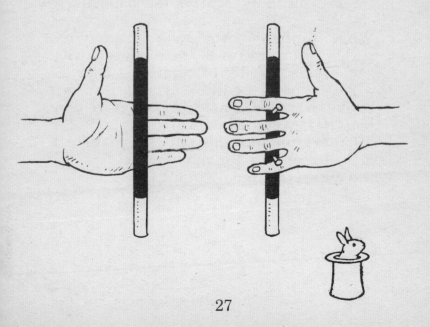

GIVE UP SMOKING!

Equipment:
    1 packet of cigarettes

What happens: You show an ordinary packet of cigarettes to the audience. You say, 'Every packet of cigarettes carries a government health warning, and we should not start smoking at all if we can help it. If we do start, we need a packet of cigarettes like this one. We just turn it the other way up, open it, and find all the cigarettes have gone!'

How it's done: Take the cigarettes out of the packet. Take out the drawer and cut it across about 2.5cm from the bottom. There will now be two pieces. These can be put back as they were. Put two or three cigarettes in the pack. On stage, push the packet up from the bottom and show the cigarettes are there, then close packet at the top, though leaving the flap out. When you announce that all the cigarettes have gone, you must lift the flap up and pull the drawer up. The bottom will stay where it is and support the cigarettes, but the drawer will come up empty.

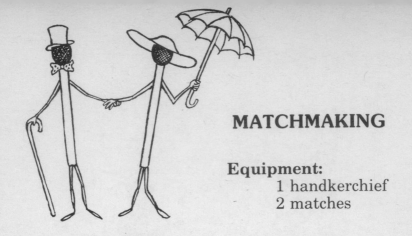

MATCHMAKING

Equipment:
    1 handkerchief
    2 matches

What happens: You ask someone if they will come up and help you. '**Have you a match**?' you ask. '**Yes**,' they answer. (You hope—otherwise give them one from a box on your table.) Ask them to mark it so they will recognise it later. Put it in the centre of a handkerchief, fold the hanky over, and over again. Ask him to break the match, and then to break it again. You can hold it up in the hanky for everyone to feel that it's well and truly broken. You lay the hanky on the table again, open it up and show everyone the match is whole again. You shake out the hanky to show there's nothing else in it, and get your victim to verify that it's the same match as he marked.

How it's done: You need to have a big white handkerchief with a seam. The sides of the seams are usually open, and you must slip a match a little way down the seam. This is the one you let the other person break. Make sure you have the right match in your grasp when you fold the hanky!

BENDY PENCIL

Equipment:
1 pencil

What happens: You borrow an ordinary pencil from the audience. It may happen that no one has one. Have one handy, and take it to the audience so they can examine it and see that it is an ordinary pencil.

Go back on the stage, shout a few magic words such as '**Rackakadabra!**' and '**Carousel!**' wave the pencil about and it will turn to rubber.

How it's done: This is what's called an '**optical illusion**'. The eye is tricked into seeing something that isn't true. This optical illusion is created by holding the pencil between your thumb and first finger about 2cm from the end and gently moving your hand up and down while holding the pencil quite loosely.

31

THE AMAZING
EXPANDING
ROPE

Equipment:
> 2.5 metres of rope

What happens: You come on stage with piece of rope in your hand. It isn't very long—about 30cm. You say, '**It would be very useful if this rope were longer—perhaps if I say the magic words, it will grow....** '**Rope-a-ca-dabra, riddle and stretch!**' The rope now expands until it's 2.5 metres long!

How it's done: This is an effective simple trick. If you glance at the diagram you can see the secret—you put the rope along your arm, then put on your jacket:

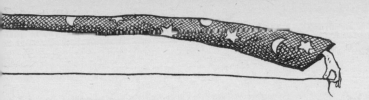

Keep the longer side of the rope
towards your other hand, so
you can '**stretch**' it easily.
If the rope is so long
that it falls down
your back you
can put it in
your inside
pocket.

33

THE AMAZING BALANCING CIGAR

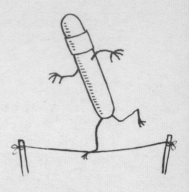

Equipment:
> 1 old hat
> 1 cigar

What happens: You have a large cigar on your table. You show it to the audience for them to see there's nothing unusual about it. You show them the hat and prove there's nothing inside it. Now, putting the hat on your left hand, you take great care in balancing the cigar upright on top of the hat. All at once you take your hand away from the cigar and move it to the brim of the hat. You move the hat around as if making a great effort to balance the cigar. The cigar stays upright, swaying a little as the hat moves about.

How it's done: You have a small, fair
blunt pin in your left hand. When you pu
the hat on your left hand, hold the pin up
so it goes through the top of the hat. Now
you can put the cigar on top of the pin, and
not only keep it upright but also make it
move as you wish it to.

THE SCARF TRICK

Equipment:
3 scarves

What happens: This is a simple trick that may flummox the cleverest member of your audience. It's also a good item to have up your sleeve if anyone in the audience is trying to be clever by calling out 'Seen it before!'.

When you have your victim on stage, you show them the three scarves. Two of the scarves are tied together with a knot. You ask the other person to put the third scarf between the two others without tearing them, and without undoing the knot.

How it's done: It's done very simply—by tying the third scarf to the ends of the other two!

WET CASH

Equipment:
    1 coin
    cotton wool

What happens: You borrow a coin from someone in the audience. You say, 'This is odd! This coin feels damp...let me see, yes, it is very damp. Look!' You press it hard and some drops of water fall from it.

How it's done: Find a paper clip and bend it to form a hook. You can dig this into your table cloth on stage and keep your ball of wet cotton on it until you do the trick. The cotton wool ball should be a little smaller than the coin. Stand behind the table with the coin, and while you're talking, bring your free hand up to pick the cotton wool off the hook. Move the coin to your other hand, pressing it against the cotton wool until water seems to drop from the coin. You will need to practise holding the cotton wool and the coin so that the coin hides the wool entirely.

BALANCING ACT

Equipment:
- 1 10p coin
- 1 glass
- 2 identical forks

What happens: You ask the audience to help you—if they can! Can anyone get a 10p piece to stay on the edge of a glass using two forks? The coin must not be supported from below. It must be made to balance on the edge. It sounds impossible, but it can be done

How it's done: Hold one fork in each hand, put their prongs together, back to back. Put the coin through the top space between the prongs. You'll find you can balance the coin on the side of the glass. As long as the forks are exactly the same weight it will stay there forever—or until someone knocks it off!

KNOTTY HANKY PANKY

Equipment:

  1 large handkerchief or teacloth

What happens: You ask if there is any-one in the audience who thinks he can tie a knot in the handkerchief. When someone comes forward, you add 'Oh, I forgot. **You have to begin with your arms folded**!' If he still wants to try it's not very likely he'll get anywhere except into a tangle, so you show him how to do it.

How it's done: Fold your arms and pick up the ends of the hanky or cloth. You'll have to stretch a bit to get the ends but you'll find that the 'knot' in your arms is transferred to the hanky when you unfold your arms.

SPOT THE SPOTS

Equipment:
  1 pack of cards

What happens: Ask someone to pick six cards from a pack of cards. You explain that the court cards count as ten, and the rest count as whatever number of spots they have. He must look at each, putting them downwards one after the other. As he puts each down, he notes its number and puts more cards on top of it from all the cards that are left, to make the total number up to twelve. So, if he sees the number is six (it doesn't matter which suit) he puts it face down and puts six more cards on top. You should be out of the room while he is doing this. You come back in, and ask for the rest of the cards so you can put them on the table while you think. You put the cards down, hold your hand to your head in deep concentration, then tell him the total of the spots of the bottom cards of the six heaps. If he hasn't already memorised this number, get him to count them up now to see if you are right.

How it's done: When you return and take the cards from him, chat for a little while so you can count the remaining cards. Put them down, and add to the number of cards left the number **26**. This will give you the total of pips on the cards at the bottom of the six piles. If there aren't enough cards left to complete the six piles, ask him how many more he needs. **Subtract** this number from **25**. You will have the answer.

PERPLEXING PAPER

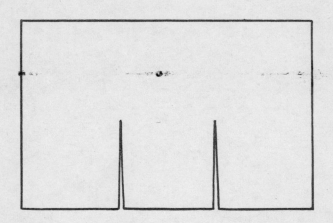

Equipment:
　　1 piece of paper

What happens: Cut a piece of paper like this:

Each of the three segments are the same size. Now ask someone in your audience to pull the two side pieces so that he tears the paper into three. However he pulls, the paper will always tear into two.

How it's done: However you pull, there will always be a bit more pull on one side than the other, so it's one of those impossible little tasks that you can give to someone in the audience who wants to come up on stage and show how clever he is!

STRANGE ORANGE

Equipment:
    1 hat
    1 orange
    1 apple

What happens: You show the audience an ordinary orange. You then show them the inside of the hat. There's nothing in it, and you pull out the band inside to show there's nothing there, either. You put the orange in the hat, feel around a bit as if you're looking for something else, then with a shout of triumph, you pull out...an apple!

How it's done: You carefully peel an orange so the peel is in two neat halves. The apple is hidden inside the orange peel. Although you can show the hat at close quarters, you must show the orange to the audience from behind your table. You can do it quickly, as they won't expect that there's anything unusual about the fruit, only about the hat.

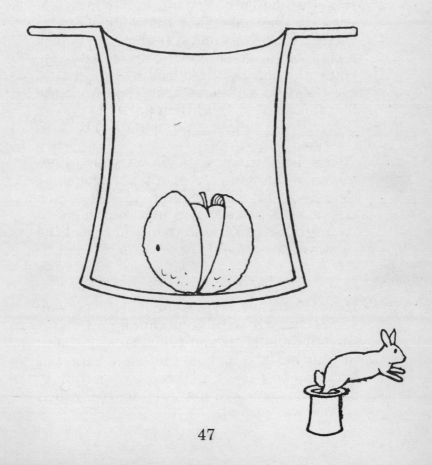

COLOUR BLIND

Equipment:
    1 box of wax crayons
    1 blindfold

What happens: You ask for an assistant from the audience. You ask him to blindfold you. He then goes into the audience with the box of crayons and gets someone to pick a crayon. He takes the crayon back to you, you feel it, all the time looking upwards so there can be no doubt about how well the blindfold is tied. You then pass the crayon back to your helper, and he puts it back in the box.

The assistant now takes off your blindfold. You announce that after a moment's thought, you will be able to say which crayon was picked. You put your hand to your forehead to think, then you reveal the colour of the crayon.

How it's done: When you feel the crayon, scrape it a bit with your thumbnail. After the blindfold is off and you raise your hand to your head, you should let your hand fall back to chest level, glance at your thumbnail, and you will be able to see which crayon was picked.

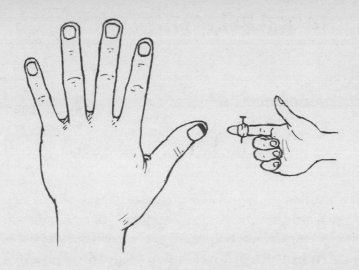

It's a good idea to use crayons which cannot be confused. Use obvious colours—yellow, blue, red, brown, orange, green—rather than risk mistaking one shade of blue for another.

THE DANCING EGG

Equipment:
- 1 egg
- 1 glass
- Air-tight covering

What happens: You tell the audience that you are going to make an egg **dance**! The egg is in a covered glass and when you push the cover down a little, the egg gets up!

How it's done: Make a hole in each end of the egg with a ball-point pen or something similar. Blow out the white and yolk. Put the egg in a glass or jam jar, then seal it with some cellophane or anything that will make the container air-tight. When you push this down, air will be forced into the hollow shell making it move about.

MAGIC MONEY

Equipment:
    Several envelopes
    1 plate

What happens: You show the audience some ordinary envelopes. They are all sealed and you say, '**In one of these is a pound note. I have six envelopes here, so I'd like five people to come and choose one each, then I'll have the last one!**' The five choose their envelopes carefully, swopping one for another until they're satisfied. You must ask them not to feel the envelopes, as this would be unfair. When they open their envelopes they find a little note saying,

    You take the last envelope, open it, and out comes the £1.

How it's done: You have the six envelopes on a plate. You have a pound note under the plate, hidden between the plate and your fingers.

After they have taken their envelopes, push the last one under your thumb while they're opening theirs. When you take this envelope, take it off the plate using your thumb, at the same time slipping the note beneath it. Tear open the envelope with your other hand. You can now pretend to find the money inside the envelope. It will fool everyone if you take the note from the back of the envelope as long as it's done smoothly, without any fumbling. Try it in front of a mirror.

WATER IN THE TOPPER

Equipment:
　　1 top hat
　　2 plastic cups

What happens: You say that every magician can pour water into a top hat—such as the one on the table. All he does is put a cup inside. At this point, show the audience that your hat is empty. Then put it on the table and place a plastic cup inside. Tell your audience that the average conjuror would simply pour water into the cup, but that you're different—you really are going to pour water straight into the hat. You remove the cup, and then pour water straight into the hat! Then you announce you'll get the water from the hat into the cup. You put the cup back in, bring it out full of water, and take the hat to the audience for them to see it is completely dry.

How it's done: Cut the bottom off one paper cup. It should now fit comfortably inside the other, but on stage it should not look any different. When you put the cup in the first time, you are really putting in both cups. When you remove the cup for the first time you only take out the bottomless cup. You must hold this with your hand covering the bottom so the audience cannot see that the bottom is missing. Then you pour water into the other cup in the hat, put the bottomless cup back inside the other and bring both out.

THE CLEVEREST BOTTLE

Equipment:

1 clear bottle
1 small circle of clear plastic

What happens: You show the audience a bottle. It's an ordinary bottle and if they like they can come up and fill it with water, and empty it again. You tell them that though they can empty it, which is quite clever, you can do something much cleverer, which is to keep the water in the bottle even when the bottle's upside down. When they are all sitting comfortably, you fill the bottle with water, turn it upside down, and they will be astonished to see that no water comes out.

How it's done: Keep the small plastic circle in your hand and put it over the top when you've filled the bottle with water. Keep it in place as you turn over the bottle and it will stay in place, keeping all the water in the bottle. Practise this over a sink. It's important that you wet the plastic with your finger before you put it on the bottle. You'll find that one or two drops of water come out as you turn the bottle over, but because of the air pressure from beneath, the plastic circle will not fall.

GOOD GUESSING

Equipment:
2 dice

What happens: You give someone two dice and ask him to give them a good shake, then stack them one on top of the other. You look away while he does this, but then you turn back and tell him the total number of spots on the three sides which are hidden.

How it's done: Glance at the number on the top of the top dice and take it away from 14. This is such a quick trick that you can do it again if you feel the mood is right, otherwise you can do another trick which requires the help of someone from the audience and ask the person if he'll help a second time. This way, there won't be such a gap between tricks.

DISAPPEARING ERASER

Equipment:
    1 rubber eraser

What happens: You hold a long thin rubber eraser in your hand, its top sticking out of the top of your fist. You cover it with a hanky and invite several members of the audience to feel that the eraser is still there. You take away the hanky immediately after the last person has checked the eraser to show everyone that it has completely disappeared!

How it's done: This requires a friend in the audience! He is the one who feels the eraser last, and takes it with him! It isn't a good idea to have a number of tricks that involve this sort of '**cheating**' but one or two add to the variety of the magic, and you and your friend can have a good laugh at your own cleverness afterwards!

THIS IS YOUR CARD

Equipment:
　　1 pack of cards

What happens: You offer someone the pick of the pack of cards. He takes a card, remembers it, and puts it back on top. You cut the pack, and tidy them. You fan out the pack, and announce the chosen card!

How it's done: Before you begin, secretly snatch a glance at the bottom card of the pack. Remember it.

Your victim puts his card on top of the pack, and you cut from the bottom to the top. Now the bottom card will have become the one before the chosen card, so when you fan out the pack you can easily see which is his card.

THE BALANCED PENNY

Equipment:
    1 1p piece
    1 glass
    1 long strip of paper

What happens: You lay a penny on top of a piece of paper which is on top of a glass:

You announce that you are going to get the paper away from the glass, leaving the penny on the glass edge.

How it's done: Hold the end of the strip of paper with your left hand. Give the paper a sharp slap with your right hand and whip the strip of paper away.

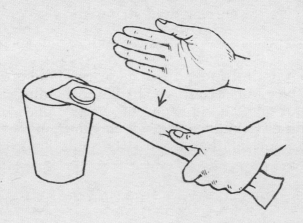

After you've practised for some time you should be able to get the penny to stay on the edge of the glass every time you try the trick.

NO STRINGS ATTACHED

Equipment:
    1 long piece of string
    1 short piece of string

What happens: You show the audience a piece of string which you're holding in your right hand. You put the two ends together to make a loop which you then move to your left hand, with the ends hanging loose:

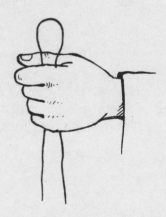

You pull up the loop so it stands clear of your hand, then you ask an adult to come up on stage and, with some scissors, cut off the top of the loop, so the string is in two. Push the two ends into the top of your fist.

62

Make some magic passes over your hand and announce that the string will reappear in one piece. Ask the adult to pull the strings at the bottom and out will come the string in one piece.

How it's done: You have two pieces of string and you keep the shorter in your left hand so that, when you transfer the longer one to your left hand, it is actually the loop of the smaller one that you pull out. The strings of the longer one hang below.

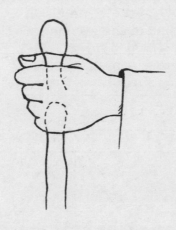

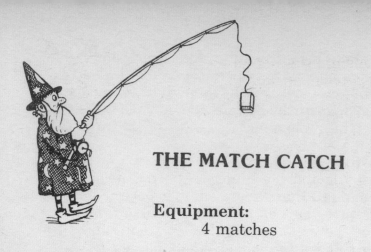

THE MATCH CATCH

Equipment:
    4 matches

What happens: Arrange three matches as below. Make a notch in the top of one, put the end of the second into the notch, and rest the third against the other two. You should have a pyramid shape:

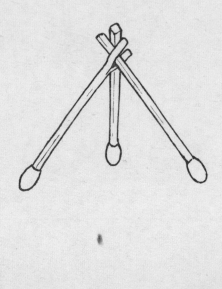

If you get this set up properly—and you'll need to try it out—the matches will stay up by themselves. You challenge anyone to pick up the three matches with a fourth.

How it's done: You put the fourth match behind the third and in front of the first two:

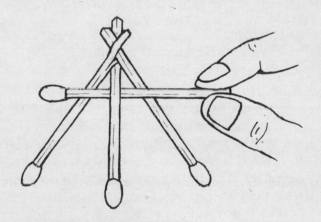

CATCHING
THE FOOL

Equipment:
    1 blackboard and chalk

What happens: This is a useful little trick to use when you need to deal with a troublesome member of the audience. Once in a while you will find a know-all who's **'seen it all before'** and the only way to keep him quiet is to get him on stage to do something very difficult, if not impossible.

Invite your noisy victim to join you and explain that you're going to ask him to do something very simple just to show everyone how clever he is. If he asks what it is, tell him you are going to ask him to write down a number on the blackboard, and that's all!

When he strides up, ask him to write on the blackboard '**Eleven thousand, eleven hundred and eleven**', in figures

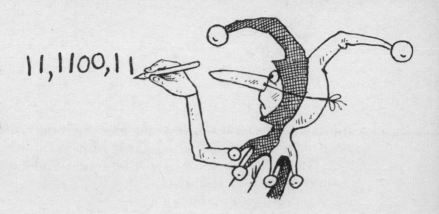

How it's done: It's even harder working this sort of thing out on stage, so there won't be much chance of him coming up with the right answer, which is: **12,111**

DIGGING OUT THE DIAMOND

Equipment:
    1 pack of cards

What happens: While you leave the room your assistant lays out ten cards on the table. They are the 1 to 10 of diamonds and he lays them out like this:

The assistant gets one of the audience to come on stage. This person has to choose a card. The assistant tells the audience which card has been picked.

When this is done, you come back on stage and tell the audience that by looking at the bottom card of the rest of the pack—which, as everyone has seen, has been on the table all the time, and has not been touched—yes, by looking at the **bottom card** of the pack, you will reveal the chosen card.

Your assistant passes you the pack, bottom up. You glance at it as he passes it, and you immediately reveal which card was chosen.

How it's done: The bottom card of the pack must be a ten. When your assistant passes you the pack he must have his thumb on the pip (the heart or the spade or the club) which is in the same position in relation to the other pips on the card as the card on the table is in relation to the other cards on the table.

A VANISHING PENNY

Equipment:
  1 1p coin

What happens: You make a 1p piece disappear by rubbing it into the back of your left hand.

How it's done: For this trick, you need to be wearing trousers with turn-ups. (And if you don't have any trousers with turn-ups, just turn up the bottoms of any trousers you do have!) You take the coin, hold it up so the audience can see it, then put it behind your left hand. Rub it round with your right hand, and then pretend to drop it by accident. Apologise as though you're very embarrassed, and when you're picking the coin up quickly drop it into your trouser turn-up, but don't change the way you have your hand. It must look as if you're still holding the coin. You pretend to go on rubbing the coin until it suddenly vanishes.

MAGIC PLASTIC

Equipment:
    1 plastic 'glass'
    1 paper clip
    1 book

What happens: You put the plastic container on a book. You turn the book the other way up. The clear plastic container is seen to hang from the book without any support.

How it's done: Bend an ordinary paper clip so one limb is at a right angle to the other. When the glass is put over this it forms a catch that holds the glass against your thumb.

WATER IN—COLA OUT!

Equipment:
    Large plastic jug
    1 paper cup
    Dish cloths

What happens: Wouldn't it be nice (you say) if it were possible to turn ordinary tap water into a delicious soft drink?

You pick up a glass of water and pour it into a jug. Straightaway, you pick up the jug and pour...out comes cola!

How it's done: Put enough dish cloths in the jug to absorb the glass of water. Fill the plastic cup nearly to the brim with cola, and make a space in the cloths just in front of the spout of the jug so you can fit the cup of cola in the jug, and the cola will pour out normally. The cloths will absorb the water you pour in.

Don't let the audience see inside the jug—
make sure that it's quite high up.

Use a drink like cola rather than a fruit
juice—the fruit juice could easily be in the
bottom of the jug before you start, but the
cola appears to be produced magically.

THE LEANING
GLASS
OF WATER

Equipment:
> 1 glass of water
> 1 matchstick

What happens: You can do this trick and do some talking at the same time. '**You've heard of the Leaning Tower of Pisa,**' you say, '**Well, this is the Leaning Glass of Water, and it's even more amazing...!**' You tip the glass over, and it stays as it is— leaning at an amazing angle.

How it's done: Put a matchstick under the cloth on your table. You can balance the glass against this if you're careful. Try it out a few times before attempting it on stage preferably with a mop and bucket nearby!

NIMBLE NUMBERS

Equipment:
None.

What happens: Ask your volunteer to think of a small number. Ask him to double it. Now he must **add 4 and divide by 2.** Then take away his original number. You tell him the answer's **2.** He will agree.

How it's done: This is real number magic because it works with any small numbers:

$$4 \times 2 = 8 + 4 = 12 \div 2 = 6 - 4 = 2$$

INK
AND
WATER
JINX

Equipment:
1 glass of water
A dip-stick
Black paper
A scarf

What happens: There is a glass of ink on your table. You put the stick in to show the audience it really is ink. The stick goes in white, and comes out black. You put a scarf over the glass of ink, say some magic words, such as '**Indelible Indian Ink!**', and whip the scarf away to reveal that you have changed the ink into water.

How it's done: The dip-stick is white on one side and black on the other. Cut the black paper so it fits the inside curves of the glass perfectly. Make sure the corners fit exactly, otherwise the illusion will not work. The black paper must come near to the top of the glass, then you can fill the glass with water up to the top of the paper and it will look like a glass of black ink.

On stage, put the dipstick in with its white face towards the audience. As you stir the ink, turn the stick round so that you bring it out with the black face towards the spectators. When pulling the scarf off the glass, put your thumb in a little so you take out the paper as well as removing the scarf, which should immediately be screwed into a ball and put away. This should be done above the eye-level of the audience.

NOW YOU HEAR IT—
NOW YOU DON'T

Equipment:
    1 matchbox
    1 coin

What happens: You take a matchbox from your pocket. You shake it to show there are matches in it, then you remove the matches. You take a coin, put it in the matchbox. Shake it, then open the matchbox to show that the coin has disappeared.

How it's done: You make a small slit in the drawer of the matchbox:

Just as you stop shaking the matchbox you should start talking— it doesn't matter what you say as long as you distract the audience for that split second when you tip the coin out of the matchbox. You can then shake the matchbox again with your right hand, while you rest your left on the table—and quietly get rid of the coin.

RISE, OH MATCH BOX!

Equipment:
    1 matchbox

What happens: You have a matchbox flat on the back of your hand. You give the command for it to rise, and—like an obedient slave—it rises up!

How it's done: Empty the box of its matches. Close it just behind your knuckles so that you have a little bit of your skin inside the box (this isn't as painful as it sounds!). If you're right-handed, put it on your left hand, and vice versa. You can have your fingers a little clenched and the box will still be flat. If you clench them a little more, (and give the command!) the matchbox will rise up.

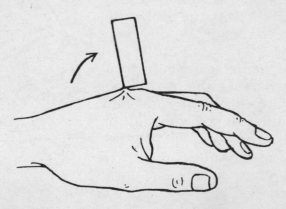

THE LEAPING EGG

Equipment:
  1 egg
  2 glasses

What happens: You have two glasses in line. In the one nearest you is an egg. You blow into the glass and the egg leaps from the first glass into the second.

How it's done: You make a hole at each end of the egg, using a ball-point pen or anything with a small, blunt point. Blow out the contents of the egg, both the yolk and all the white, until the shell is empty. Now it will be very light, and you will find it requires little puff to make it go from one glass to the other.

THE JUMPING WAND

Equipment:
   1 wand

What happens: You're holding the wand upwards in your hand, and talking. The wand keeps trying to move up and out of your hand, but you push it down, saying, **'Stay there!'** Finally it leaps right out of your hand, but you catch it with your other one!

How it's done: You hold the wand in your left hand. Around your middle finger, wear a **rubber band**. The bottom of the wand rests on this rubber band, but the wand is held by you so you can decide how far it moves about and exactly when it is going to leap from your hand. The audience only sees the front of your hand. Catching the wand is something you'll just have to practise!

80

THE IMPOSSIBLE MOVE

Equipment:
None

What happens: This is a good little item which will silence the know-all. If you have a difficult audience you can get more than one person to try doing the impossible move. Line them all up so they have their right shoulders against a wall. '**All you lot have to do,**' you tell them, '**is what the simplest person in the world ought to be able to do—lift your left leg.**' Try as they might, they won't be able to do it without taking their shoulder away from the wall.

How it's done: You need to be able to change your balance when you pick up your leg, but with the wall there, this becomes impossible. If anyone asks you how it's done, you'll have to admit that it **isn't**!

CAN YOU DO IT?

'82

Equipment:
1 mug
1 piece of paper

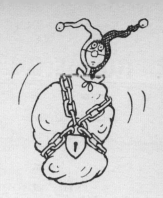

What happens: You ask for assistance from a member of the audience. When you have someone, put an old mug on a piece of paper so that the end of the paper hangs over the side of the table. Ask him to get the paper away from the table without touching the mug, and without overturning it.

How it's done: Your victim will probably try to pull the paper out quickly, so it's a good idea to have carpet underneath so that when the mug drops it won't break! The proper way to do it is to bang the table hard with your right hand, and at the same time remove the paper with your left. The jolt will make the mug leap, so you have to be quick, but it **will** work!

THE MILE OF THREAD

Equipment:
   1 reel of cotton

What happens: This is as much a joke as a proper trick, but it makes for a very funny interlude between more serious items, and it's even something you can do during another trick. Get someone to come up on stage. Begin a trick with him, say, with cards. Then you notice there's a bit of thread hanging from his shirt. You say, '**Let me pull off that bit of thread for you**.' You pull and pull. It doesn't stop, and you both end up with armfuls of thread.

How it's done: You must prepare this beforehand with the person who comes up on stage. Just get a small reel with a lot of cotton on it, put it inside his shirt in the bulge of shirt at the top of his trousers, put the end of the thread through a button hole, and you can keep pulling until all the cotton on the reel is used up!

TRICKY HANKY

Equipment:
    1 coin
    1 handkerchief
    1 rubber band

What happens: You put a handkerchief over your hand and ask someone to place a coin on it. You take the hanky off, shake it, but the coin has gone!

How it's done: Around your fingers and thumb, double a tight rubber band. Put a large handkerchief over your hand and make a small pocket in the middle of it with your finger. It's into this that the coin will go. This pocket will be over the palm of your hand. The rubber band is around the handkerchief, but not touching it. When the coin falls or is placed on the handkerchief, let the rubber band go. It will hold the coin in place so that when you shake the handkerchief the coin won't show, and won't fall out.

A MAGIC TURN

Equipment:
1 pack of cards

What happens: Someone from the audience helps you. He takes a card from the pack, looks at it, then puts it back in the pack. You go and lay the cards out on a table **face-down**. One card will be **face-up**—the card your victim chose!

How it's done: Turn over the bottom card of the pack before you begin. Spread out the cards a little, so he can see they're all the right way up, but make sure the bottom card is hidden. When he's looking at the card he's taken, turn the pack over without him or any of the audience seeing. This must be done quickly, and will require some practice for you to be able to do it smoothly. It's best if you can do it with one hand, and do something else with your other to distract the audience's attention—like scratching your head very deliberately. After he's put the card back in the pack, you turn to the table. At this point you must quickly turn the bottom card over again so it's facing the same way as all the others. Now when you spread the cards, only one will be facing the wrong way, and this will be his.

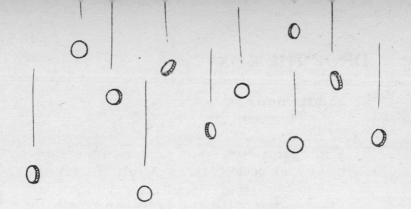

PENNIES FROM HEAVEN

Equipment:
    1 glass
    2 coins

What happens: You hold a glass. You grab a coin out of thin air and throw it into the glass. It drops to the bottom. In case any one missed it, you do it again!

How it's done: When you hold your empty glass, hold it by the rim with two fingers inside and your thumb against the outside. Under these two fingers you have two small coins. You can chatter about finding money in the air, looking for it, and suddenly catching it with your free hand; as you make the motion of throwing the coin in the glass, let one of the coins go so it falls to the bottom of the glass just at the moment a coin would have done had it really been thrown in there by your other hand.

DROP THE BOX!

Equipment:
    1 matchbox

What happens: You produce a matchbox from your pocket, throw it into the air and it lands with its label-side up. '**Ah**!' you say, '**It's landed with the label up. Well, I'll do it once again. Which way up is it this time? The same again!**'

Now the box will always land with its heavier side downwards, so you can choose before you start the side you want to have landing upwards. Don't forget to choose a matchbox that has different designs on its back and front! Of course, if you do have one with the same designs, the trick will work without the coin—but the audience may not be amused!

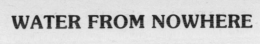

WATER FROM NOWHERE

Equipment:
>1 specially adapted jacket
>1 small plastic beaker with top
>1 large handkerchief

What happens: You show your audience the large handkerchief. There's nothing in it, back or front. You throw it casually over your left arm, and when you take away the handkerchief a glass of water has appeared in your hand. As the audience cheers, you say '**Cheers!**' and drink the water.

How it's done: For this, you need to be good with a needle, or you'll have to get someone who is to help. On an old jacket stitch a breast pocket on the left side, a little nearer to the arm than usual, and a little lower. Into this goes the small plastic beaker, filled with water, and covered with its tightly-fitting top. When you throw the handkerchief over your left arm, put your right hand under the hanky and quickly remove the top of the beaker, and at the same time get the beaker out of the hidden pocket using your little finger of your left hand at the beaker's base to ease it up into the thumb and forefinger of your left hand. You can now whisk away the handkerchief—with the plastic top hidden inside— and show the beaker of water to the audience. And you prove it is really water by drinking it.

THE FLOATING NEEDLE

Equipment:
  1 glass of water
  1 needle

What happens: You show your audience
an ordinary glass of water. You hold up an
ordinary needle and announce that you are
going to make it float on the water even
though everyone knows steel should sink.

How it's done: You must have a needle
that's completely dry. It's best if you wipe
the needle with a dry cloth before you start.
Getting the needle to float calls for a steady
hand. The needle must rest flat upon the
surface of the liquid where it is supported
by the film on the water, so you will need
to try this out quite a bit before getting the
hang of it.

CIGARETTE MAGIC

Equipment:
1 cigarette

What happens: You borrow a cigarette from an adult member of your audience. You put it on a table where everyone can see it. You lick a finger, and make a magic circle round the cigarette. Then, lick a finger on the other hand and make a path from the circle you've drawn towards yourself. Both these 'lines' should be drawn on the surface of the table. When you point a finger at the cigarette, it will roll away from you.

How it's done: The drawing of the circle and the path is just a bit of misleading nonsense. When you point at the cigarette, you blow very gently without altering the shape of your lips. You must not have anything else on the table which might be blown about so giving the game away. Though this may sound an unconvincing trick in print, it fools everyone who doesn't know the secret, as long as you draw the circle and path convincingly, and don't let them see that you're blowing.

COINS FROM NOWHERE

Equipment:
    A dozen coins
    Some wax

What happens: You have some coins and you give them to the audience to count. When they have agreed as to how many coins you have, you take them back and put them down on the table. You say, '**Now, just to make sure I'll count them**...' You sweep them off the table into your hand, count them and discover there's more than there were before. You can let the audience check this. You try again. There's more again!

How it's done: At the back of your table, just under it's edge, you have a few coins kept in place with wax or blu-tac. If you use blu-tac you can experiment to find the best way of using it—probably the best way is to put quite a large lump on, and press the coin lightly against it.

Whichever you use, your table should look something like this:

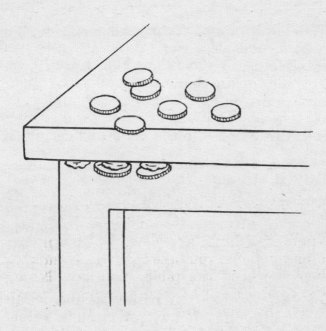

When you take the coins from the audience the first time, you can put them down on the table quite naturally, and talk about how difficult it is to save money nowadays. Then you go on to say that you want to make sure the number of coins is the same, and hasn't got smaller since you put them on the table. As you pull the coins into your waiting palm, you can use one of your fingers to flick the coins off the underside of the table and into your hand.

THE INCREDIBLE
MIND READER

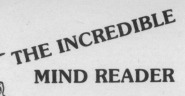

What happens: Your assistant holds up a coin, and asks you what it is. You are blind-folded, but you are able to tell him. He holds up another coin—a different one— and again you tell him correctly what it is. Now he holds up a note of some value. You tell him he's holding a pound note, and so on.

How it's done: You tell what note or coin your assistant is holding by the words he uses. If he says '**WHAT am I holding**?' you know it's a note. If he says, '**HOW much is this worth**?' you know it's a coin. His answer to your '**guess**' will tell you the actual value of the note or coin. When you've guessed whether it's a note or a coin, he can give four replies that will give you its value:

YES = 1p or £1
YUP = 5p or £5
THAT'S IT = 10p or £10
CORRECT = 50p or £20

This leaves—**½p and 2p**, for which you can have, say, '**Good**'—meaning ½p—and '**Exactly**', which means he's holding a **2p** piece. Once you've memorized this, you can not only use coins from your table, but ask the audience to give coins to your assistant for him to reveal 'telepathically' to you what they are!

94

MAGIC SUGAR

Equipment:
>   1 cup of tea
>   2 lumps of sugar

What happens: Get the audience to gather round the cup of tea you have on the table. Tell them that you are going to say a few magic words—**'Teapotty strainer and magic cosy!'**—and the sugar cube will float on the surface of the tea until it dissolves.

How it's done: Do this at the beginning of a show. The tea should be cold. Put the first cube in before the show starts, then when you put the second in, rest it on top of the other. If you find the cube dissolves before you can get the second one in while you're rehearsing, try holding the other in the palm of your hand. You can keep it hidden until you try to balance the second. Drop it in while holding the other cube with the thumbs and first fingers of both hands.

A FISTFUL OF WATER

Equipment:
 1 paper cup
 1 shallow dish

What happens: You fill the paper cup with water. You put it in the shallow dish as you announce—while rolling up your sleeves—that you're going to pour all the water into your fist. You proceed to do this, but then you say the magic word '**Drought!**', open your fist and show the astonished audience that the water has disappeared. There are a few drops there, proving that the water did run into your fist.

How it's done: Near the bottom of the cup is a small hole. When you fill the cup with water, keep your finger over this hole. The water will run out when you put the cup in the shallow dish except for a little below the hole. This is what the audience sees when you begin to pour. You can turn slightly so that they see the first few drops going in but then see just the cup being tipped slowly up. If you do this smoothly you can create a very good illusion.

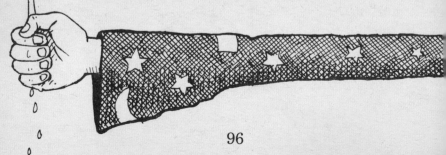

THE RICH ROLL

Equipment:
　　1 bread roll　1 5p piece

What happens:　It's one thing to find six-
pence in your Christmas pudding, but here
you show the audience an ordinary bread
roll, break it open and there will be 5p inside!

How it's done:　When you hold the roll,
bend the ends upwards so there's a little
break in the bottom. Push the 5p into this
break. When you break the roll, break it so
the centre comes up and you can push the
5p into the heart of the bread. Then you can
put your fingers in and produce it, as if it
had been in the roll all along.

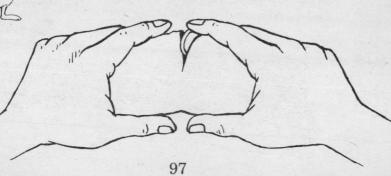

CRAFTY CUTTING

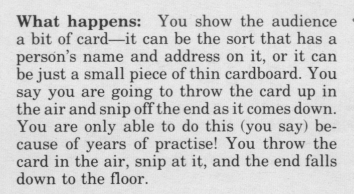

Equipment:
>Some card
>1 pair of scissors

What happens: You show the audience a bit of card—it can be the sort that has a person's name and address on it, or it can be just a small piece of thin cardboard. You say you are going to throw the card up in the air and snip off the end as it comes down. You are only able to do this (you say) because of years of practise! You throw the card in the air, snip at it, and the end falls down to the floor.

>**How it's done:** The scissors can be blunt! It's probably a good idea to use blunt ones— they'll be safer. All you do is cut the end off the card before you begin and put it between the scissor blades. When you clip the paper, that is, when you pretend to cut it, snip very quickly and the card in the scissors will be released as the blades are opened. It will seem as if you really have cut the end off the card.

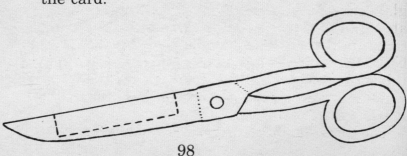

SLIM COINS

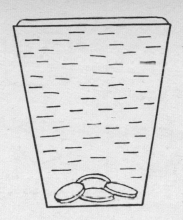

Equipment:
    1 glass of water
    4 coins

What happens: You fill a glass of water to the brim. You tell the audience, 'It would be impossible for me to put another drop of water in this glass without it overflowing.' If you like, you can get someone from the audience to fill it to the brim. You then drop four coins in, one after the other pointing out, with mounting concern, that the water still hasn't overflowed!

How it's done: The coins must be dropped in very carefully, and the outside of the glass must be completely dry. You'll probably find that you can drop more than four coins in, but experiment will give you the best idea of how many to use and how full the glass can be. As the coins go in, the water rises above the top of the glass but it still doesn't overflow.

    The coins should be dropped in sideways.

99

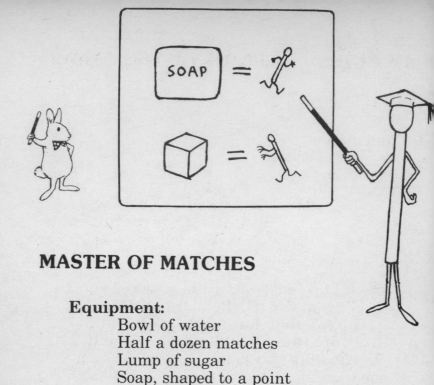

MASTER OF MATCHES

Equipment:
      Bowl of water
      Half a dozen matches
      Lump of sugar
      Soap, shaped to a point

What happens: You tell the audience that you are going to master the matches, if they would like to gather round the table and watch. You put the matches in a circle on the surface of the water in the bowl. Leave a space that's about the size of a penny in the centre of the ring of matches. Put in the soap, and the matches will flee to the side of the bowl. Put the sugar cube in the centre and hold it. All the matches will return to the centre of of the bowl.

How it's done: There's no trickery here—it's a bit of '**real magic**' that's brought about by the surface tension of the water.

GENIUS OF THE CARDS

Equipment:
    1 pack of cards

What happens: You ask someone to choose a card and not to show you what it is. You tell them which card they have taken.

How it's done: There's a code that must be learnt before you can perform this startling trick. The code goes like this: **6, 4, Ace, 7, 5, King, 9, 10, 8, Jack, 3, Queen, 2.** Once you've memorised this, remember **Clubs, Hearts, Spades and Diamonds.**

You arrange your pack so it follows this code, that's to say, **6 of Clubs, 4 of hearts, Ace of Spades, 7 of Diamonds, 5 of Clubs, King of Hearts, 9 of Spades, 10 of Diamonds, 8 of Clubs, Jack of Hearts, 3 of Spades, Queen of Diamonds, 2 of Clubs, 6 of Hearts, 4 of Spades, Ace of Diamonds, 7 of Clubs and so on.** When you offer the person the pack, and he picks a card, put the rest of the pack on the bottom. The bottom card will be the one that was above the card chosen and because you know how the cards run, it's possible to tell the person which card they chose. If the card on the bottom is the 4 of Hearts you know his card is the Ace of Spades.

101

COIN FROM NOWHERE

Equipment:
    1 coin
    1 candle

What happens: On your table you have an ordinary candle. You say something along the lines of '**Wouldn't it be nice if money came out of thin air? Of course it doesn't but sometimes it seems to**...' While you chatter away your hand passes up and down the candle, and suddenly you have a penny in your hand.

WOULDN'T IT BE NICE IF MONEY CAME OUT OF THIN AIR?

How it's done: Do not light the candle. There is no need and it will interfere with the trick. If it seems odd that you have a candle which isn't alight, just say something like, **"Of course, in these hard times we must save all the energy we can, so I haven't lit the candle**...' In the back of a candle make a small slit before you begin the show. Put the coin in, and do the trick a few times. Each time you'll have to push the coin in a bit deeper, but you'll get a good idea of how far in to push it so it will stay put before the trick, but come out of the candle easily when you grasp it.

This is, of course, another piece of '**sleight of hand**'. As your hand passes up and down the candle, you get closer to the coin, and quickly grasp it with the base of your thumb and first finger. With practise, you can bring the coin forward to between the tips of your thumb and fingers to show it to the audience

HATCHING THE MATCHES

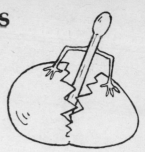

Equipment:
    A box of matches

What happens: You show the audience an empty box of matches. You close the box, say a few magical words, open the box and show them that, out of thin air, matches have appeared.

How it's done: Put a row of matches between the drawer and the box so that when the drawer is closed the matches fall into the box. The matches are kept up by the back of the drawer, so the box is open when you first show it—you don't open it and then show it. The arrangement should be like this:

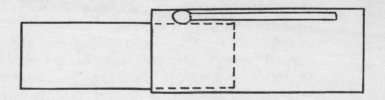

THE WANDERING WAND

Equipment:
    1 wand
    1 coloured bottle
    60cm of black thread
    White tape

What happens: You say that your wand has been very restless lately. If you put it down in one place, **it wanders about the room by itself**. Even if it's put in a bottle—such as the one on the table—it tries to get out! You put the wand in the bottle, and sure enough, it rises up until you order it down again, and keeps trying to get out until you pick it up and put it sharply down on the table.

How it's done: This is an amusing trick, but it will only work properly when it is performed at some distance from the audience, or against a dark background. The wand is pulled up by a length of thread. The thread should be attached to the wand by a small strip of white tape that goes over the white end of your wand. No one will see that this end is different from the other if you do this neatly. Tie the other end of the thread to your jacket pocket. Before you do the trick, it's best if you keep the wand in your inside pocket. You can explain that you have to keep it there, otherwise it wanders off! After the trick, a short, sharp tug should break off the thread, though you may prefer just to put the wand back in your inside pocket. That way, you won't have buttons flying about!

As you step back, the wand rises, and as you approach, it goes back into the bottle. You'll need to try out different lengths of thread to get it exactly right. You need to have the thread a little way out when you're standing over it so you can take it out easily at the end.

ONE POUND A GLASS

Equipment:
> 1 one pound note
> 1 glass

What happens: You borrow a pound note from the audience. You put the pound note under a glass and ask if anyone can get the note out from under the glass without touching the glass. If they don't know the secret, they won't be able to, though they may try to whip the note out from under the glass very quickly, in the way that people are supposed to be able to whip a table cloth off a table and leave all the crockery and cutlery exactly where it was. If they do seem to be about to do this, stop them, and say you don't want broken glass everywhere!

How it's done: The simple secret is that you roll up the pound note from the end, very tightly, keeping your hands away from the glass. The middle of the rolled note will push the glass away.

AN EGG SPINNER

Equipment:
  1 hard—boiled egg
  A few uncooked eggs

What happens: Invite a few people from the audience up on stage. You give them each an egg, and ask them to spin their egg on the table so that it stands on its end. No one, except for you is able to do it.

How it's done: You have the only hard-boiled egg. Your egg will spin on its end, but the others won't!

TELEPATHIC TURNING

Equipment:
    1 pack of cards

What happens: Along the edge of a table, you lay out in a straight line all the Kings, Queens and Jacks in the pack. The cards should be face-up. You then invite members of the audience to turn one or more of these court cards around while you are out of the room. You go out. They turn some of the cards round. You come back and tell them which cards have been turned round.

How it's done: Playing cards have one margin slightly wider than the other. When you lay the cards out, make sure you have them with the larger margin at the top. When you come back into the room you'll be able to see which have been turned round because some will now have the smaller margin at the top.

SLIM SUGAR

Equipment:
   1 wrapped sugar cube

What happens: You sit behind your table and show everyone the piece of sugar wrapped in the paper. You say, '**Here's one of those cubes you're given in cafes— the sort that drops into your tea and stays there until you've finished. They never dissolve, do they? Not only that, but they're so thin that they go right through solid tables!**' As you say this, you bring your fist down on the sugar cube. The paper goes flat and you bring the cube out from under the table.

How it's done:
Find a wrapped sugar cube and carefully unwrap one end and remove the sugar. Rearrange the paper so that it looks as if the sugar is still inside. On stage, have the sugar lump in your lap. You can show the audience the paper. Bring your fist down on the paper cube and then with your other hand bring the sugar cube from your lap from under the table.

BOTTLIN' EGGS

Equipment:
    1 egg
    Some vinegar
    1 bottle

What happens: You have an egg sitting on top of a bottle. You announce—and proceed to demonstrate—that you can get the egg inside the bottle **without breaking the shell.**

How it's done: You need to prepare this trick about a week in advance. Put the egg in some vinegar. In a few days the egg shell itself will dissolve leaving the strong elastic skin that looks very like the actual eggshell. This retains the shape of the egg, and can be gently eased into the bottle without breaking. You also need to practice!

112

BAGS THE BALLOON

Equipment:
    1 large brown paper bag
    2 balloons

What happens: You turn the large paper bag upside down. A balloon falls out. You show the balloon to the audience, then undo the knot in the top and let the air out. You put the balloon back in the bag and blow into the bag hard several times. You then put your hand in the bag and bring out the balloon, which is once again blown up.

How it's done: This is a very simple bit of magic. Have both balloons half blown up. There will then be room for both in the large bag. Stick one to the side of the bag with a small piece of sticky tape. Make sure the tape is clear and clean so that it isn't visible from where the audience are sitting. The tape should be just big enough to keep it in position but small enough not to rip the side of the bag when you pull the balloon out. The second balloon on top is, of course, the one that drops out at the beginning. It stays in the bag when you pull out the second.

113

THE MAGICIAN'S TABLE

For some tricks you will need to have a special **magician's** table, one that has a secret feature known to professional conjurors as a '**servante**'. This is a secret shelf or space at the back of your table where you can hide important bits and pieces. You can make a '**servante**' very simply by covering an ordinary small table with a tablecloth and then folding the cloth at the back up to the corners of the table so a pocket is formed. You can pin the corners up with safety pins. Another '**servante**' can be a drawer in your table. Put a piece of material at the bottom of the drawer so anything you drop in makes no noise when hitting the bottom of the drawer. You should see that the drawer cannot be seen from in front: you'll have to experiment with how far out the drawer can be pulled and at what level you have the table. If it's too high, the audience may be able to see the bottom of the drawer at the back of the table.

Using the '**servante**' will require practice. Do your tricks in front of a long mirror so you can see the best way of distracting the audience's attention, as well as seeing how good you are!

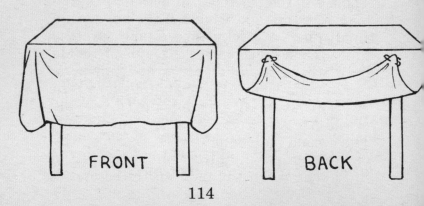

FRONT   BACK

THE TOP HAT TRICK

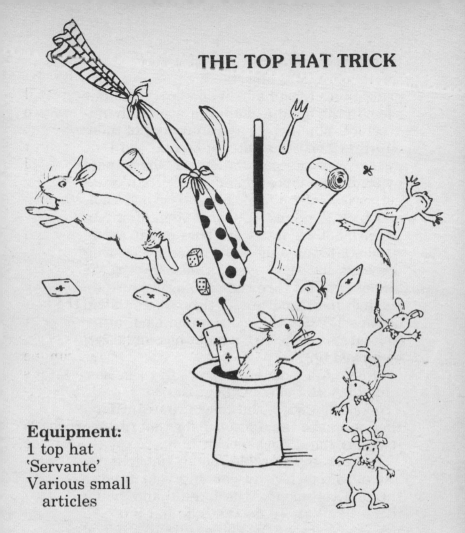

Equipment:
1 top hat
'Servante'
Various small
   articles

What happens: You show an ordinary
top hat to the audience. You lay it flat on
the table and make a few passes with your
magic wand over the hat. You turn it over,
and draw out a bar of chocolate, some
matches, a spoon, a brussel sprout, and
other things like this until at last you draw
out a large spotted handkerchief.

How it's done: You get an assortment of small household objects, such as the ones drawn out of the hat, given above, and put them in the middle of a large, spotted handkerchief. When you have a number of them which, when tied into a bundle, will fit nicely into your top hat, make the bundle by tying the opposite ends of the hanky together over the pile of things. Use one knot, and tuck the ends in. Cut a strip of strong paper, about 2.5cm wide, and put it round the bundle keeping it in place by pasting the ends together. Next, find one of those bits of covered wire that are used to tie up rubbish bags and put it through the strip of paper. Twist the ends round each other so it forms a loop with which the bundle can be picked up.

The bundle should be placed in the 'servante' before the show begins.

When you start the trick, you can hand the top hat to the audience for them to see it's empty and hasn't been tampered with. You lay it on the table, make your passes, and as you pick it up you slip your fingers through the loop of the bundle and swing it into the hat. To do this, the hat must be near the back of the table, just in front of the 'servante'.

Put your thumb on the brim of the hat, and your first finger beneath it and you can use your other fingers to pick up the bundle. It will swing into the hat quite easily. You hold the hat at a slight angle away from the audience and let go of the loop.

You have to do the next bit very quickly and smoothly, talking all the time. Your right hand darts into the hat, breaks the paper strip, undoes the knot and brings out the first object. You can then bring out all the other objects one by one—as your audience bursts into wild applause.

THE SWIVEL

Equipment:
    1 coin

What happens: You hold a coin between the first finger and the thumb of your left hand. You show the audience the back and front of the coin, and then move your right hand towards it as if you are going to take it. Pass the right fingers over it, with the right thumb under it. Close your right hand tightly to show you're holding the coin there. Wait a moment, then open your right hand to show the coin has **vanished**. Then open your left one to show that it's not there either!

How it's done: This is a very basic piece of **'sleight-of-hand'**. It requires some practice, but isn't as difficult as it seems at first, and is very effective once you have the movements going smoothly. When you pretend to grasp the coin with your right hand, let the coin slip down into the palm of your left hand. Bring the right hand up to show the audience that is where the coin is, at the same time slipping the coin from the left hand into a **secret pocket**. You can now open your right hand, and then your left, and the coin will have disappeared!

THE POSTCARD TRICK

Equipment:
  1 glass of water
  1 postcard

What happens: You say to the audience, 'I'm going to perform the impossible...once again! I am going to support a glass of water—this glass of water here—with this picture postcard. You can examine both the card and the glass of water—you can see they haven't been tampered with in any way whatsoever.' You put the card on top of the glass of water, turn the glass over, and the postcard supports the water!

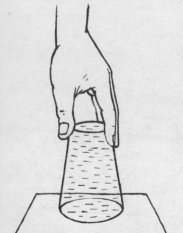

How it's done: This might be called '**real magic**'—there's no trickery; air pressure keeps the postcard in place. This is one of those tricks that do not seem possible until you try them, but it does work I promise! Find a postcard you do not want anymore. Make sure it's fairly flat. Put the glossy side on to the top of the glass, and just turn the glass over. The first time you do it, you'll feel less nervous if you hold the glass over a sink, but as you get confident, you can do it anywhere.

KINGS, QUEENS, JACKS TOGETHER!

Equipment:
1 pack of cards

What happens: You put all the Kings, Queens and Jacks together and ask some one to put them anywhere in the pack he likes. Ask him to cut the pack **twelve** times—that is, split it anywhere he likes and put the top to the bottom. Take the pack, wave your hands over it, and say that even though they have been split, you have now reunited the Kings, Queens and Jacks. When you look through the pack they will be all together.

How it's done: There's one chance in five hundred that this will go wrong, but if it does, it'll be even more effective the second time when—unless you're one of the un-luckiest people in the world—it will go right! There's no 'trick' to it—it just happens that, however he cuts the pack, the court cards stay together. To give yourself some confidence, you can try it!

WHAT A CARD!

Equipment:
    1 pack of cards

What happens: Before you begin, you put a card on the table. You invite someone up on stage and ask him which cards he would like, the red or the black. If he says the red, you can say that leaves just the black cards, that is to say, the spades and the clubs. You can now invite him to choose between the spades and the clubs. He says the clubs, so you say that you're left with just the spades. Out of the spades, would he like the high or low cards? He says he wants the low ones. You say that you're left with the high cards—the Ace, the King, the Queen, the Jack, and the ten. What would he like now? He can have the Ace, the King and the Queen **or** he can have the Jack and the ten. If he says the Ace, the King and the Queen, you say that that leaves you with the Jack and the ten. He may, of course, pick the alternative, but if you think for a moment, you can see that it doesn't matter which of the alternatives he picks, you can always steer him. Out of the Jack and ten, he may pick the Jack, in which case you say, '**That leaves me with the ten, which you will find on the table.**'

How it's done: If you go through all this quickly, it will seem very clever, but of course if you think about it, you're just guiding him to the card on the table. Whichever of the alternatives he picks, you either say, **"Well, you can choose from those . . .'** and go straight on to the next choice, or you can say **'That leaves me with . . .'** If he begins by choosing black, and the card on the table is a club, you say, **'Very well. Which of the black cards do you want, spades or clubs?'** If he picks spades, you say **'That leaves me with clubs. Which of the clubs does he want, the high ones or the low ones?'** And so it goes on until you get him to choose the card on the table, or get him to choose the other one so you can say **'Well, then ten (or whatever it is) is left for me!'** and you can pick up the card on the table and show him it's the ten.

A KNIFE IN THE PACK

Equipment:
  1 pack of cards
  1 ordinary cutlery knife

What happens: You give someone the pack of cards and ask them to choose a card. Then they must cut the pack, putting the two halves on the table. You then say '**I'm going to tell you on which half to put your card**.' You indicate which half, he puts the card on top, then you put the other half of the pack on top of the card. You announce that when you tap the side of the pack with your magic knife (or you can use anything like it—a magic wand if you have one) the pack will separate at the spot where the chosen card lies. You tap the pack and show the person his chosen card.

How it's done: You have between the finger and thumb of your right hand a very **few grains of salt**. When you indicate which pack you want him to put his card on, you drop the salt on top. When the other card and the rest of the pack is put on top of this, the deck will slide slightly. Keep it all together until the magic tapping, and let the pack slide so that the card's position is revealed. Like all the other tricks, you can try this on your own—you'll be surprised at how well it works, even with a very few grains of salt!

A HANDY GUESS

Equipment:
1 coin

What happens: Invite someone from the audience to take part in the trick. If no one is eager to take part, you can reassure them by saying that all they have to do is stand and hold a coin. When someone comes up, give him the coin. Turn your back. Now ask him to put the coin in the other hand, if he so wishes, or to keep it in the same hand, to hold it tightly and to raise whichever hand holds the coin to his forehead. After a few magic moments ask him to hold out both hands towards you, with both fists clenched so it is impossible to know for sure which hand the coin is in.

You turn round and tell him which hand the coin **is** in!

If the audience thinks this is a lucky guess, do it three times.

How it's done: The hand that holds the coin to the forehead will be **paler** than the other hand when the two clenched fists are shown to you. To give yourself confidence, try it!

CLEVER CREASES

Equipment:
    3 glasses
    1 piece of paper

What happens: You put the paper across two of the glasses. It's an ordinary piece of paper, so the audience will be puzzled when you challenge them to stand the third glass on top of the paper.

How it's done: Fold the paper into **pleats**. This strengthens the paper, and you'll be able to put the third glass on top. To make the pleats, fold the paper from the edge, turning over about 2cm, then fold it back on itself, then again as the first time.

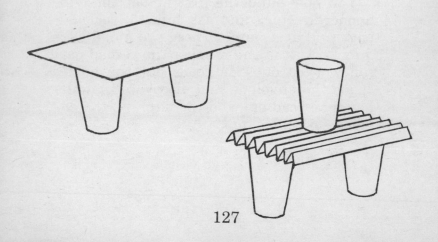

THE NUMBER SECRET

Equipment:
    1 piece of paper
    1 envelope
    1 telephone directory

What happens: You are on stage with your helper. You give your helper a sealed envelope. You ask him to call out three different numbers. You write these down. You ask someone else to come up and to make a few calculations with the numbers. When he's done this, he tells everyone the figure he's come up with.

You now hand the first helper the telephone directory and ask him to look at a page and at a name. These are found as a direct result of the number the second person worked out. He reads out the name, opens the envelope and discovers that the name he read out and the name in the envelope are the same.

How it's done: This is a trick that requires some **preparation**. Before you go onstage, look at page 108. Count to the ninth name down the page. Write this, with the forename and initials if there are any, on a piece of paper. Put the paper in an envelope. Seal the envelope.

Hand this to your first helper. When your second helper calls out three numbers, you write these down, preferably on a blackboard, or on a large sheet of paper with a felt-tip pen so everyone can see what's been written.

Now get your second helper to do some calculations. Here's an example:

The number called out is **371**.
You ask him to put this down back to front: **173**.
He then **takes away** the smaller number from the larger.

$$\begin{array}{r} 371 \\ \underline{173} \\ 198 \end{array}$$

He must put this number back to front (**891**) and add the two numbers together together:

$$\begin{array}{r} 891 \\ \underline{198} \\ 1089 \end{array}$$

This answer, **1089**, will come up which-ever numbers are used. If after the sub-traction you come up with a two figure num-ber, such as **98**, you must put a nought before it—**098**.

Ask the first helper to look in the tele-phone directory on page **108**, and to count down the left hand column until he gets to the ninth name. Ask him to tell everyone what this name is, then ask him to open the envelope he's holding and to read out that name.

The two names will be the same.

WHICH WAY WILL THE REEL ROLL?

Equipment:
Reel of cotton
Strip of board

What happens: You need to find a reel with a slim barrel, as below. You put it on an incline—you can use a small strip of cardboard—and hold it in place while you talk to your audience. '**Things are not always as they seem**,' you say, and let go of the reel. As you pull the thread the reel rolls **uphill** towards you.

How it's done: The reel touches the board and it seems as if it must roll down, but because the point at which it touches is lower than the point at which the reel is being pulled the opposite thing happens. This is one of those tricks that aren't really tricks at all, but it will astonish your audience just the same!

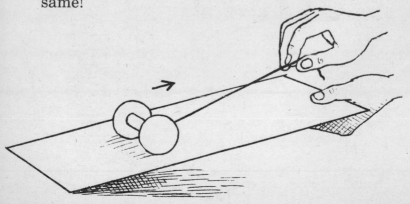

THE ENERGETIC ACE

Equipment:
    1 glass
    1 playing card

What happens: You say that you have noticed that the aces in the pack are more energetic than the other cards. Perhaps the audience thinks you are mad? Take any other card but an ace and push it into the glass. Nothing happens. Take an ace and push it in—the ace immediately rises!

How it's done: Rub a little soap on opposite sides of the glass. When you put the first card in, you put it where the soap **isn't**, and then you put an ace where the soap has made the sides of the glass slippy and the ace will rise.

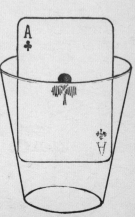

HOLIDAY SPECIAL

Equipment:
    1 map of the world
    1 pad of paper
    1 pencil
    1 hat

What happens: You tell the audience that you've saved lots of money and can go anywhere in the world (or the country, if that's the only map you've got). Ask them to suggest places for you to go. As they suggest them, write them down on bits of paper, fold them in half, then in half again and put them into your hat. Ask someone from the audience to mix up the papers for you, and then to take one out. You think for a moment, then tell everyone which place is written on the piece of paper.

How it's done: You write the first suggestion down on all the pieces of paper. If you get a suggestion that's much longer than the first, write the first place-name down and then pretend to write for a while longer, so the audience don't suspect. If it's shorter, write more quickly!

Whichever piece of paper the assistant picks, it will have the same place-name on it.

THE SWINGING BOTTLE

Equipment:
    1 dark green or brown bottle
    1 piece of thin rope or cord
    A piece of rubber eraser

What happens: You show the audience the bottle. You show them the length of cord. You put the cord in the bottle, hold the bottle up, then let go! Instead of falling to the ground and smashing, it stays where it is. Catch the bottle, and the rope comes out.

How it's done: You need a small bit of **rubber eraser**, so just cut off a small piece with rounded edges. Drop it into the bottle. When you put the rope into the bottle, hold the bottle upside down. The bit of eraser will fall into the neck and form a wedge that will keep the cord in place. You should be able to give the rope a little tug while the bottle is upside down to check this has happened. When you catch the bottle, push the cord down slightly the instant after the bottle is in your grasp. This will make the eraser drop and you will be able to pull out the cord.

134

GLASS FLIPS

Equipment:
   3 glasses

What happens: You have three glasses in a line on your table. The outside two are the right way up, but the middle one is upside down. You ask someone from the audience to get them all upside-down, in three moves, turning two glasses at a time. They'll try and try but almost certainly they won't be able to do it—until you show them how easy it is!

How it's done:
The first turn is glasses 2 and 3.
The second is glasses 1 and 3.
The third is glasses 2 and 3 again.

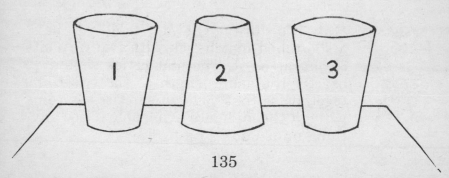

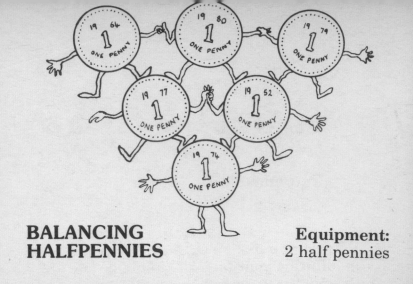

BALANCING HALFPENNIES

Equipment:
2 half pennies

What happens: You show the audience you have two ordinary ½p pieces, or you can ask them for two if you like. You say that you will balance the two, one on top of the other—but would anyone like to try before you do it? Take the coins to the audience and get someone to have a go. They are sure to drop them, so retrieve them, take them to your table and announce that you will have to lay them flat to perform this difficult feat. You pick them up from the table with them perfectly balanced between your finger and thumb.

How it's done: On your table you have a shortened matchstick with two tiny bits of blu-tac on it. The matchstick should be exactly the same length as the two coins together so that you can support the coins without the audience being able to see anything unusual.

136

DODGY DICE

Equipment:
    2 dice
    1 glass

What happens:
Hold a glass and
two dice like this:

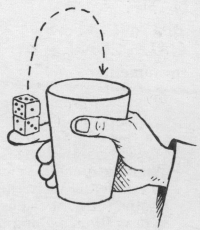

Now ask someone to come up from the audience. Give them the dice and glass and
ask them to throw the dice up in the air,
one at a time, and catch them in the glass.
The person may be able to get the first one
in, but the second will never go in without
the first one coming out again!

How it's done: When you come to do this,
get the first in, then **drop** the second dice
and **lower** the glass very quickly to catch
it.

137

WHAT'S THE DATE, MATE?

Equipment:
- 1 pad
- 2 pencils
- 1 calendar

What happens: You ask someone to choose from the calendar 3 dates which follow one another, say, 4, 5, 6, or, 24, 25, 26—any three will do as long as they are **consecutive**. They must not tell you which dates they have chosen. If the calendar is quite large, they can circle the dates and show the audience, or go down to the audience and show them which three dates have been chosen. They now add the three dates together and give you the total. After a moment, you tell everyone which dates were the ones chosen.

How it's done: You divide the total by **3**. This will give you the middle date. Subtract 1 to get the date before it, and add 1 to get the date after it.

138

THE CHARMING COMB

Equipment:
  1 towel
  1 cotton reel
  1 paper cup
  1 comb

What happens: With an Indian turban (or an ordinary towel!) round your head, you can charm a snaky thread hanging over the side of a paper cup, making it rise and follow your comb.

How it's done: Before you begin, rub the comb round and round on your sleeve, all the time mumbling mystic words. By rubbing, you create **'static electricity'** and this will stay in the comb for a while after you've stopped rubbing. When you move the comb over the thread, the thread will be attracted by the static electricity, and will sway around like a snake.

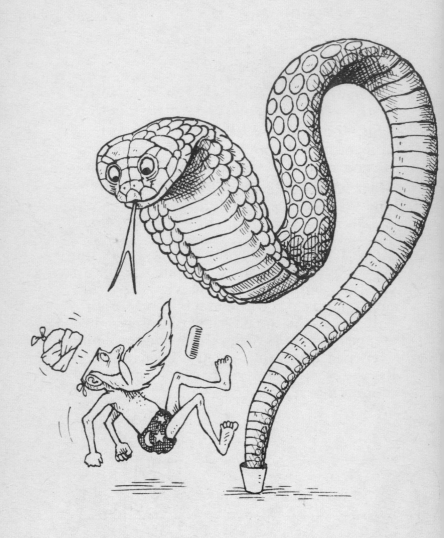

THE LAST STRAW

Equipment:
1 bottle
1 straw

What happens: You invite someone from the audience to help you. You want to lift up the bottle using just one straw—can they do it for you?

How it's done: Bend the end of the straw over and put the bent end into the bottle. It will now stick in the neck and you'll be able to pick the bottle up using just the one straw.